Rest as Resistance: A Work-Life Balance Book for Gen Z and Millennials

A Themed Essay Collection on the Anti-Hustle Movement, Burnout Recovery, and the Radical Act of Putting Yourself First

Jordan R Sloane

Contents

Introduction: The Lie We Bought Into — v

Part 1
The Origins of Hustle Culture

1. The American Dream 2.0 – Work Until You Drop — 3
2. The Rise of the 24/7 Grind – From Wall Street to Instagram — 5
3. You Are Your Job – How Work Became Our Identity — 9

Part 2
The Psychological Cost of Hustle Culture

4. The Productivity Trap – Are We Working More, But Getting Less Done? — 17
5. The Anxiety Economy – Why We're Always One Step from Panic — 22
6. The Burnout Generation – Millennials and Gen Z vs. Work — 28

Part 3
The Systemic Issues Behind Hustle Culture

7. The Corporate Wellness Scam – When Self-Care is a Productivity Tool — 37
8. The Gig Economy Trap – Freedom or Just More Exploitation? — 48
9. Who Wins from Hustle Culture? (Hint: Not Us) — 54

Part 4
The Future of Work and Rest

10. The Anti-Hustle Movement – How We're Fighting Back   63
11. Rest as Rebellion – The Radical Act of Doing Nothing   69
12. Redefining Success – What Comes After the Grind?   74

Conclusion: The Death of Hustle Culture?   79

Introduction: The Lie We Bought Into

I remember the exact moment I realized hustle culture was a scam. It wasn't during an all-nighter fueled by cheap coffee and ambition, nor was it when I hit a so-called milestone—an impressive job title, a five-figure project, or the coveted "hustler" badge of honor. It was at 3 a.m. on a Tuesday, staring blankly at my laptop screen, my inbox flooded with urgent-but-not-really emails, my heart racing from too much caffeine and too little sleep.

I had done everything I was supposed to do. I had internalized every success mantra: "Sleep is for the weak." "You have the same 24 hours as Beyoncé." "Grind now, rest later." And yet, there I was—exhausted, anxious, and questioning why, despite all my efforts, I felt more like a machine running on fumes than a person building a fulfilling life. That was the moment the cracks in the narrative became impossible to ignore.

Hustle culture is everywhere. It's in the airbrushed success stories plastered across LinkedIn, the relentless grind

Introduction: The Lie We Bought Into

showcased on Instagram, and the motivational speeches urging us to push past exhaustion, to work harder, faster, longer. It's in the offices where working late is a badge of honor, where responding to emails at midnight proves your dedication, and where "self-care" is just another way to optimize productivity. It's in the gig economy's promise of freedom that disguises itself as self-exploitation. It's in the startup world's obsession with "disrupting" industries while quietly burning out its workforce. It's in the insidious belief that our worth is measured by our output.

The myth of hustle culture is built on grand promises: work hard enough, and success is inevitable. Put in the hours, and you'll make it. Grind nonstop, and the rewards will be limitless. But the reality is far messier. Hustle culture doesn't just demand our labor; it demands our identity. It convinces us that rest is failure, that slowing down is weakness, that if we're struggling, we just need to push harder. It sells us a dream while quietly extracting every last ounce of our energy, time, and well-being. And for whom?

This book is about breaking down the myth of hustle culture, piece by piece. We'll examine where this obsession with overwork comes from, how it evolved into a mainstream ideology, and who actually benefits from keeping us exhausted. We'll explore the psychological toll of constantly chasing productivity, the systemic forces that fuel our burnout, and why stepping away from the grind isn't just necessary—it's revolutionary. We've been told that success requires sacrifice. But what if the greatest trick hustle culture ever pulled was convincing us that the sacrifice was worth it?

Let's dismantle the lie together.

Part 1

The Origins of Hustle Culture

"Hustle culture didn't just sell us hard work—it sold us the illusion that exhaustion is a badge of honor, that sleep is for the weak, and that if we're struggling, it's because we're not grinding hard enough. But the truth is, no one is 'failing' at hustle culture—hustle culture is failing all of us."

Chapter 1

The American Dream 2.0 – Work Until You Drop

Hustle culture didn't appear out of nowhere. It is deeply rooted in historical, economic, and ideological systems that have shaped the way we think about work, success, and self-worth. To fully understand why we're all running on empty, we need to go back—way back—to the foundations of overwork.

The Historical Roots of Overwork: Puritan Work Ethic, Industrialization, and Capitalism

From the early days of American society, hard work has been equated with moral virtue. The Puritan work ethic instilled the belief that productivity was not just necessary for survival, but a sign of righteousness. Over time, this philosophy evolved to fit the needs of industrialization, where long hours of labor became the backbone of economic progress. As capitalism took hold, the value of a person became increasingly tied to their output, shaping a culture where rest was seen as laziness and overwork was glorified.

How the "Rags-to-Riches" Narrative Fuels Toxic Productivity

The American Dream, a concept built on the idea that hard work guarantees success, has been both an inspiration and a trap. The stories of self-made millionaires and bootstrapped entrepreneurs reinforce the idea that anyone can make it—if only they grind hard enough. But what these narratives often ignore are the systemic barriers that make upward mobility far from accessible to everyone. By placing the burden of success solely on the individual, hustle culture keeps people locked in a cycle of endless striving, convinced that failure is always a personal shortcoming rather than a result of structural inequities.

The Shift from Survival Labor to Identity Labor: Work as Self-Worth

In the past, work was primarily a means of survival. But in today's world, particularly in white-collar industries and the gig economy, work has become an identity. Careers are no longer just a way to pay the bills; they are a reflection of who we are. The pressure to be passionate about our jobs, to turn hobbies into side hustles, and to constantly optimize productivity has led to a culture where people feel guilty for resting. The line between personal fulfillment and professional obligation has become so blurred that many no longer know who they are outside of their work.

Chapter 2

The Rise of the 24/7 Grind – From Wall Street to Instagram

The Cult of Endless Work

It's 2 a.m., and somewhere in Silicon Valley, a startup founder is tweeting about how sleep is for the weak. Across the world, an influencer is posting about how they "never stop hustling," accompanied by a carefully curated photo of a laptop, an oat milk latte, and a scenic view. The message is clear: if you're not grinding, you're falling behind.

Hustle culture didn't start with social media, but tech has certainly perfected it. What began on Wall Street—the glorification of overwork, the badge of honor that comes with pulling 80-hour weeks—has now seeped into every industry. The tech world, in particular, has played a pivotal role in rebranding workaholism as a virtue. Figures like Elon Musk, who famously said, "Nobody ever changed the world on 40 hours a week," have become icons of this relentless, all-consuming grind.

But what they don't tell you is that the people pushing this mindset are often the ones who benefit the most from it.

The Tech Industry and the Myth of Passion-Driven Work

Silicon Valley has long marketed itself as a utopia for the ambitious. It's a place where 20-somethings code in hoodie-clad brilliance, fueled by Red Bull and an unwavering belief in their startup's world-changing mission. Companies like Google and Facebook transformed the workplace, introducing nap pods, unlimited snacks, and ping-pong tables—not as acts of generosity, but as strategies to keep employees in the office longer. The workday doesn't end when your shift is over; it bleeds into your social life, your identity, your very sense of purpose.

The tech world romanticizes overwork by framing it as a privilege: "You're not just working—you're building something revolutionary." But behind the ping-pong tables and kombucha taps, burnout is rampant. Employees at top companies routinely report crushing hours, the expectation to be "always on," and the quiet shame that comes with admitting they need a break.

Then there's the startup world, where the dream of being your own boss often turns into a nightmare of constant work. The idea that founders must sacrifice their health, relationships, and sanity for success is deeply ingrained. Investors reward those who appear the most devoted, the ones who seem willing to go without sleep, vacations, or even basic human needs. But this level of overwork isn't a sign of dedication—it's a sign of systemic exploitation disguised as ambition.

The Influencer Economy and the Illusion of Passive Income

If Wall Street and Silicon Valley pushed hustle culture in the corporate world, social media amplified it for the masses. The rise of influencers, entrepreneurs, and online business moguls has created an entirely new version of the grind—one that promises financial freedom but often delivers endless labor.

The influencer economy is built on the myth of passive income: the idea that if you work hard now, money will eventually flow in while you sleep. Instagram and TikTok are filled with "success stories" of people who left their 9-to-5s and now make six figures working from the beach. What they don't show is the relentless content creation, the algorithm changes that tank engagement overnight, the pressure to be constantly visible.

The hustle never really stops. If you're not creating content, you're irrelevant. If you're not selling a course, a product, a service, you're leaving money on the table. Even rest becomes something to monetize—self-care isn't just about unwinding, it's an opportunity to sell a brand partnership with a meditation app.

And the worst part? Most people never actually make it. The influencer economy thrives on a small percentage of winners and a vast majority of hopefuls grinding for a payout that may never come. It's not a roadmap to success; it's a lottery, and most people don't hit the jackpot.

The Blurred Line Between Ambition and Exploitation

Hustle culture thrives on the promise that hard work leads to success. But at what point does ambition become self-exploitation? The 24/7 grind is not about passion or innovation—it's about extracting as much labor as possible while convincing people that exhaustion is a virtue.

Tech billionaires glorify overwork while quietly outsourcing their most grueling tasks. Influencers sell the dream of financial freedom while spending every waking hour maintaining their digital persona. The entire system is designed to make people feel like they're always one step behind—because if they ever stopped to question it, they might realize that the game is rigged.

The real winners of hustle culture aren't the ones pulling all-nighters or sacrificing their well-being. They're the ones at the top, profiting from everyone else's exhaustion. And until we challenge the narrative, the cycle will continue.

It's time to stop glorifying burnout. The 24/7 grind isn't a badge of honor—it's a trap

Chapter 3

You Are Your Job – How Work Became Our Identity

When Did "What Do You Do?" Become "Who Are You?"

Go to any social gathering, and one of the first questions you'll be asked is: *So, what do you do?* Not *what do you love?* Not *what makes you happy?* Not *what's the last thing that made you laugh so hard you cried?* Just: *What do you do?*

In a world obsessed with productivity, our jobs have become more than just a means to pay the bills—they've become our identities. Our self-worth is measured by our LinkedIn titles, our value dictated by how much we produce, and our existence reduced to a résumé. We don't just work jobs anymore; we *are* our jobs.

But this isn't how it's always been. Somewhere along the way, the idea that work is just something you do to survive became an outdated notion. Now, work is something you're supposed to love, something you're supposed to be *passionate* about, something that should define you. And if you don't feel that way? Well, that's a *you* problem.

So how did we get here? And more importantly—how do we get out?

The Cult of Personal Branding and the Monetization of the Self

Once upon a time, having a job meant clocking in, doing your work, and clocking out. Now, thanks to the rise of personal branding, you're expected to curate a professional persona that extends far beyond your actual work. Social media has turned every industry into a marketplace, and we're all walking advertisements for our own labor.

LinkedIn is a prime example—what was once a simple networking site has become a platform for humblebrags, self-mythologizing, and the constant pressure to prove that you're always *leveling up*. Every achievement must be turned into a story of resilience, every mundane task reframed as a lesson in leadership.

And it's not just traditional jobs. The expectation to brand yourself bleeds into creative fields, too. Writers aren't just writers; they need newsletters, social media followings, and an online "presence" to be taken seriously. Artists are expected to market themselves, build a recognizable aesthetic, and engage with followers to maintain visibility. Even therapists, chefs, and teachers are now encouraged to cultivate a personal brand.

It's exhausting. And worse, it makes *everything* feel like work.

The constant pressure to market yourself turns your identity into a product, your life into content, and your passions into commodities. You're not allowed to simply *be*—you have to be *valuable*.

The Side Hustle Epidemic: Turning Every Hobby into a Revenue Stream

Hobbies used to be things you did for fun. Reading a book, painting a picture, baking cookies, playing an instrument—activities that existed purely for joy, for relaxation, for personal fulfillment. But in today's hustle-driven world, if you're not making money from it, you're *wasting potential*.

Love knitting? Start an Etsy shop. Enjoy playing video games? Have you tried streaming on Twitch? Good at photography? Better start selling presets. Even something as simple as journaling has been turned into a monetizable skill—why just write for yourself when you could start a Substack and build an audience?

Social media reinforces this mindset. Every time you see a post that says, *"If you're good at something, never do it for free,"* the underlying message is clear: your time, your skills, your creativity should always be generating income.

Of course, there's nothing wrong with making money off something you love. The problem is when the expectation to monetize turns joy into obligation. Once a hobby becomes a side hustle, it's no longer about personal enjoyment—it's about algorithms, engagement rates, and profit margins.

And if your hobby doesn't generate income? It starts to feel like a waste of time.

Which brings us to the ultimate lie hustle culture has sold us: the idea that **rest is laziness**.

Why Doing Nothing Feels Wrong (Spoiler: It's Capitalism)

Picture this: It's a Sunday afternoon, and you finally have time to relax. You could take a nap, go for a walk, watch a show. But instead, a small, nagging voice in the back of your head says: *You should be doing something productive.*

That voice? That's capitalism whispering in your ear.

Hustle culture has conditioned us to believe that our worth is tied to our output. Rest is only acceptable if it's "earned." If you're not actively producing something—whether it's work, content, or personal growth—you're failing.

Even self-care has been repackaged into a productivity hack. Meditation apps exist not to help you relax, but to *optimize* your focus. Sleep is now a tool for "better performance." Exercise isn't just about feeling good—it's about *grinding* toward a better, stronger, more disciplined version of yourself.

We don't know how to just *be* anymore. Every moment must be maximized, every action justified. Even vacations aren't safe from the hustle mindset—if you're not using your trip to network, gain inspiration, or take aesthetic photos for content, are you really making the most of it?

But here's the truth: **rest is not laziness. It's necessary.**

The idea that we must constantly be productive is not natural—it's a construct designed to extract as much labor from us as possible. The people at the top don't follow these rules. Billionaires preach hustle while outsourcing their most tedious tasks. The wealthiest people in the world have the luxury of leisure, while the rest of us are told to "grind harder."

If work was truly the key to success, then the hardest-working people—teachers, nurses, delivery drivers, janitors—would be the richest among us. But they're not. Because hustle culture was never about rewarding effort—it was about control.

Reclaiming Identity from Work

So what happens if we separate self-worth from productivity? If we stop measuring our value by how much we accomplish?

Maybe we'd find out that we are more than what we do for a living. That our lives have meaning outside of work. That joy, rest, and leisure are not luxuries, but rights.

The world won't fall apart if we step off the treadmill. Work will always be there. But who we are—outside of our jobs, our brands, our hustle—is worth rediscovering.

Part 2
The Psychological Cost of Hustle Culture

"Burnout isn't a personal failure—it's a system failure. We were never meant to be endlessly productive machines, yet hustle culture convinces us that exhaustion is proof of ambition. The real rebellion? Choosing to rest, refusing to apologize for it, and realizing that our worth has never been tied to how much we produce."

Chapter 4

The Productivity Trap – Are We Working More, But Getting Less Done?

The Modern Obsession with "Getting Things Done"

We love to measure productivity. How many emails did you send today? How many hours were you "in the zone"? Did you check enough things off your to-do list to justify your existence?

Hustle culture has turned productivity into a moral virtue. If you're not constantly working, optimizing, or improving, you're wasting time. The goal isn't just to get things done—it's to get them done *faster*, *better*, and *without ever stopping*.

But here's the thing: despite all the time-management hacks, Pomodoro techniques, and "rise-and-grind" mantras, we're not actually getting more done. If anything, we're getting *less* done—but at a much higher personal cost. The reality is that our obsession with productivity is a scam. We're working longer hours, pushing ourselves harder, and yet, we're more exhausted, distracted, and inefficient than ever.

So what went wrong?

. . .

The Myth of Multitasking and the "Always-On" Culture

For years, we were sold the lie that multitasking was a superpower. Juggle multiple projects at once! Answer emails while sitting in meetings! Squeeze in work between bites of lunch! The more you can do at the same time, the more valuable you are—right?

Wrong. Studies have repeatedly shown that multitasking doesn't make us more productive—it makes us *worse* at everything we're doing. Switching between tasks slows us down, increases mistakes, and drains mental energy. Our brains aren't wired to focus on multiple complex tasks at once, no matter how much corporate culture wants us to believe otherwise.

But modern work culture doesn't just demand multitasking—it demands we be *constantly* available. The expectation to be "always on" means that even when we're technically off the clock, we're never *really* off.

Slack notifications at 9 p.m. Emails labeled *URGENT* at 6 a.m. Unspoken pressure to reply to messages *immediately*—because if you don't, someone else will. Work has seeped into every moment of our lives, blurring the lines between professional and personal time.

And instead of questioning this system, we've internalized it. We wear busyness like a badge of honor, bragging about our packed schedules as if exhaustion is a status symbol. But the truth is, no one is thriving in this system—not even the people who seem to be.

Why Constant Work Actually Kills Creativity

Creativity—real creativity—requires space. It needs boredom, downtime, and moments of quiet. Some of the greatest ideas in history came not from grinding, but from stepping away.

Newton didn't discover gravity while grinding out reports in an office—he was *daydreaming* under a tree. Countless artists, writers, and inventors have credited their best ideas to long walks, naps, or moments of rest.

Yet hustle culture treats rest like a weakness. We've been conditioned to believe that if we're not actively working, we're wasting time. But the science says otherwise:

• Studies show that people who take regular breaks are more focused and productive than those who grind non-stop.

• Sleep-deprived brains struggle with problem-solving and creative thinking.

• Taking time off leads to *better* work—not just more of it.

The irony? The very thing hustle culture discourages—rest—is the *key* to doing meaningful work.

The Paradox of Burnout: When Working Harder Makes Us Less Effective

We push ourselves to the limit, thinking that if we just work *a little bit harder*, we'll finally catch up. But instead, we hit a wall. We get stuck in cycles of exhaustion, frustration, and inefficiency.

Burnout isn't just about feeling tired. It's a full-body shutdown—a state where your brain stops cooperating, your motivation disappears, and even the simplest tasks feel impossible. And the worst part? The more burned out you are, the *less* effective you become.

- You make more mistakes.

- You take longer to complete tasks.

- You lose the ability to think clearly.

Burnout is the ultimate betrayal of hustle culture: we are told that the more we work, the more successful we'll be. But in reality, the more we push ourselves past our limits, the less we actually accomplish.

So why do we keep falling for the trap?

Because the system is built this way.

Corporate culture thrives on burnout because exhausted workers don't have the energy to fight back. The more overworked we are, the less we question unfair workloads, unpaid overtime, and toxic work environments. Hustle culture convinces us that *we* are the problem—that if we're struggling, it's because we're not working *hard enough*, rather than acknowledging that the system itself is broken.

Breaking Free from the Productivity Illusion

So how do we escape the productivity trap? How do we break the cycle of overwork and burnout?

1 Stop equating busyness with success. Just because you're constantly doing something doesn't mean you're achieving anything meaningful.

2 Take breaks—real ones. Step away from work, go for a walk, let your mind wander. Your brain *needs* downtime.

3 Set boundaries. Work will take as much of your life as you allow it to. Protect your personal time like your well-being depends on it—because it does.

4 Redefine productivity. Instead of measuring success by how much you get done, start valuing the *quality* of your work—and your life.

Because at the end of the day, the goal shouldn't be to squeeze every last drop of energy out of ourselves. The goal should be to build a life where we don't have to choose between doing good work and actually *living*.

The real productivity hack? Learning when to stop.

Chapter 5

The Anxiety Economy – Why We're Always One Step from Panic

Why Does It Feel Like We're Always Running Out of Time?

It's midnight, and you're lying in bed, staring at the ceiling, running through the endless mental to-do list: *Did I finish that email? Will I ever get a raise? Am I working hard enough? What if I lose my job?*

This is what hustle culture does—it keeps us on edge, always a little bit behind, always convinced that if we just *work harder*, we'll finally reach some kind of safety. But that safety never comes, because the system is designed to keep us *afraid*.

Fear is a powerful motivator. And in the modern economy, fear—of job loss, of falling behind, of not being good enough—is the engine that keeps us grinding. We are constantly told that we're one step away from failure, that security is a privilege we have to *earn*, and that the only way to stay ahead is to *never stop working*.

But let's be honest: the hustle doesn't actually *protect* us. It just keeps us exhausted, anxious, and too busy to question why we feel this way in the first place.

Hustle Culture Thrives on Insecurity

The modern workforce runs on fear. Fear of layoffs. Fear of not keeping up. Fear of falling behind in an economy where everything—from rent to healthcare to groceries—is getting more expensive while wages stay stagnant.

For decades, job security was something people could count on. You got a job, you worked hard, and in return, you had stability—benefits, pensions, a future. But today? Stability is a luxury. Full-time jobs are increasingly replaced by contract work, gig jobs, and "flexible" employment (which is really just code for *no benefits, no protections*).

And the more unstable our jobs become, the more we internalize the idea that if we fail, it's *our* fault.

Hustle culture tells us that success is a choice, that if we're struggling, it's because we're not working hard enough. But the truth is, many of us are working harder than ever, and it's still not enough. The goalposts keep moving:

• *Work hard, and you'll be successful!* (But wages aren't rising.)

• *Build your skills, and you'll stay competitive!* (But industries are shrinking.)

• *Start a side hustle, and take control of your income!* (But most side gigs barely cover the bills.)

The message is clear: *If you're anxious about money, work harder. If you're burned out, push through. If you're struggling, it's because you're not doing enough.*

But let's be real—no amount of hustle will fix an economic system built to keep people on edge.

Workplace Anxiety and Imposter Syndrome: The Constant Fear of "Not Enough"

Even for those with stable jobs, the anxiety doesn't go away. If anything, it gets worse. The pressure to *prove yourself* never stops.

Many of us—especially millennials and Gen Z—grew up being told that we had to be exceptional just to survive. Good grades, extracurriculars, internships, networking, personal branding—it was never enough to just be competent. You had to be *the best*, or else risk being left behind.

This mindset carries over into the workplace, where imposter syndrome runs rampant. No matter how skilled or experienced we are, many of us still feel like we're *faking it*, constantly waiting for someone to realize we don't actually belong.

And why wouldn't we? The modern workplace thrives on competition and artificial scarcity:

• Job postings demand "rockstars" and "ninjas" instead of regular, capable employees.

• Companies foster hyper-competitive environments, where you're constantly evaluated against your peers.

- Raises and promotions are framed as rare, special rewards—something to be *earned* through sacrifice, not a basic acknowledgment of your work.

So we overwork. We say yes to extra projects. We answer emails on weekends. We never take time off, because we're afraid of seeming "replaceable." And in the process, we destroy our mental health.

The Connection Between Overwork, Stress, and Declining Mental Health

Hustle culture doesn't just make us anxious—it's physically and mentally wrecking us.

- Chronic stress from overwork is linked to depression, anxiety, and even cardiovascular disease.

- The pressure to always be "on" has led to a spike in workplace burnout, with symptoms ranging from emotional exhaustion to complete mental breakdowns.

- The rise of remote work has blurred the line between personal life and work life, leaving people feeling like they *never* get a break.

And yet, instead of addressing the root causes of workplace stress, companies hand out "mental health initiatives" like stress management workshops and mindfulness apps—conveniently ignoring the fact that *the job itself* is what's making people sick.

Corporate wellness programs are not designed to help workers—they're designed to keep them *functional enough* to keep working. Because if companies truly cared about mental health, they wouldn't just offer yoga sessions and therapy discounts. They would offer:

- **Higher wages** (so people aren't constantly stressed about money).

- **Reasonable workloads** (so employees don't feel like they have to work 60-hour weeks to keep up).

- **Real job security** (so workers don't live in fear of layoffs).

But those changes would cost money, so instead, we get emails about "self-care" and reminders to practice gratitude while we drown in unrealistic expectations.

Breaking Free from the Anxiety Economy

Here's the hard truth: hustle culture will never give us the security we crave. It will keep us working harder, faster, longer—but it will never make us *feel safe*.

So how do we step off the hamster wheel?

1 Recognize that insecurity is a feature of the system, not a personal failing. You're not anxious because you're lazy or inadequate—you're anxious because the modern workforce is designed to keep people on edge.

2 Challenge the idea that work = self-worth. Your value is not tied to your productivity. You are more than your job title, your income, or your output.

3 Set boundaries, even when it feels uncomfortable. Stop glorifying overwork. Close the laptop. Say no. The system won't change overnight, but you can choose not to let it control every part of your life.

4 Demand better. Fair wages, humane working conditions, actual job security—these aren't unreasonable asks. They're the *bare minimum* for a functioning society. The more we collectively reject the myth that endless hustle is the only path to success, the closer we get to building something better.

Because at the end of the day, the biggest scam of hustle culture is the lie that working yourself into the ground will ever make you feel safe. It won't. The only way to escape the anxiety economy is to stop playing its game.

Chapter 6

The Burnout Generation – Millennials and Gen Z vs. Work

Burnout Isn't a Personal Failing—It's a System Failure

Millennials and Gen Z didn't invent burnout, but we sure did perfect it. We're the first generations to be told, *"Do what you love and you'll never work a day in your life,"* only to realize that in practice, this actually means, *"Love what you do or you'll be left behind."*

We were raised with a promise: that if we worked hard, stayed in school, and followed the rules, we'd be rewarded with stable jobs, comfortable salaries, and the elusive dream of financial security. Instead, we graduated into economic crashes, housing crises, stagnant wages, and skyrocketing living costs. We watched previous generations build wealth through affordable education and homeownership, while we drowned in student debt and rising rent.

So, what did we do? We adapted. We leaned into the grind. We took on unpaid internships, juggled multiple side gigs, and convinced ourselves that if we just worked hard enough, we'd catch up.

And then we burned out.

Not because we were weak. Not because we didn't try hard enough. But because the system was never built for us to win.

Burnout Isn't an Individual Problem—It's a Structural One

For years, burnout was treated as a personal issue, something to be "managed" through better time management, morning routines, and self-care rituals. But burnout isn't just about working long hours—it's about working long hours *without seeing progress*. It's about feeling like no matter how much effort you put in, you're still running in place.

A generation ago, working hard meant building a future. Now, working hard just means *surviving*.

- **Wages haven't kept up with inflation.** Many millennials are earning the same (or less) than their parents did at the same age, despite being more educated and more productive.

- **Housing is unaffordable.** Millennials and Gen Z spend a significantly higher percentage of their income on rent, with homeownership feeling like a distant dream.

- **Job stability is a joke.** Gone are the days of staying with a company for 30 years and retiring with a pension. Today's workers are expected to jump from job to job, constantly "upskilling" just to remain employable.

Burnout isn't just about being *tired*—it's about feeling like no matter how hard you push, you'll never reach solid ground. And when exhaustion meets hopelessness, something breaks.

That's what we're witnessing now.

Who Gets to Rest? The Privilege of Opting Out

One of the biggest myths of hustle culture is that *anyone* can step back if they just prioritize better. But not everyone has that luxury.

The conversation around burnout often focuses on knowledge workers—tech employees, journalists, creatives—who have the privilege of choosing when to unplug. But what about the workers who *can't* afford to step away?

- The gig workers who drive, deliver, and hustle because if they take a break, they don't get paid.

- The retail and service workers who are expected to be "grateful" just to have a job.

- The parents working multiple jobs just to keep food on the table.

Hustle culture doesn't hit everyone equally. Rest is a privilege. The ability to reject the grind—to "quiet quit," to take mental health days, to push back against toxic work environments—is a luxury that many simply can't afford.

And yet, despite this imbalance, something is shifting.

• • •

The Consequences: Mass Resignations, Quiet Quitting, and Changing Work Values

For decades, the expectation was simple: work hard, don't complain, and be grateful for your paycheck. But something snapped in the last few years.

Enter: **The Great Resignation.**

During the last few years workers across industries walked away from their jobs—not because they didn't need them, but because they were *done*. Done with being underpaid, overworked, and unappreciated. Done with toxic workplaces that demanded everything and gave nothing in return. Done with a system that expected infinite output with no investment in worker well-being.

And for those who didn't outright quit? There was **quiet quitting**—a silent rebellion against hustle culture. Quiet quitting isn't about being lazy or doing the bare minimum—it's about refusing to go above and beyond for companies that don't value their employees. It's about working *exactly* as much as you're paid for, no more, no less.

The reaction to this shift was predictable. CEOs and corporate leaders panicked, calling workers "entitled" and "unmotivated." But was it really entitlement? Or was it just the first real pushback against a broken system?

Millennials and Gen Z aren't rejecting work itself—we're rejecting **exploitative** work. We're demanding better pay, fairer treatment, and jobs that respect work-life balance. We're realizing that the hustle isn't worth it if it comes at the cost of our health, our happiness, and our futures.

. . .

What Comes Next?

Burnout was never meant to be a lifestyle. The fact that an entire generation is exhausted, disillusioned, and pushing back against traditional work culture isn't a sign of failure—it's a sign of evolution.

The old model is crumbling, and something new is emerging:

• **Flexible work arrangements.** Remote work, four-day workweeks, and hybrid schedules are becoming more common.

• **Worker solidarity.** Unions are making a comeback, and labor strikes are forcing companies to rethink their treatment of employees.

• **A shift in priorities.** Success is no longer just about climbing the corporate ladder—it's about finding a balance that allows people to actually *live*.

But change doesn't happen overnight. As long as companies profit from burnout, they'll keep pushing hustle culture. And as long as economic instability keeps workers desperate, the grind will remain the default.

So where do we go from here?

1 Keep rejecting toxic work norms. The more people push back—through quitting, unionizing, or simply refusing to overwork—the harder it becomes for companies to ignore.

2 Redefine success. The goal shouldn't be to work ourselves into the ground. It should be to build lives where work is just *one* part of who we are—not our entire identity.

3 Fight for systemic change. Real change won't come from self-care routines and burnout recovery tips—it will come from better labor laws, fair wages, and a cultural shift in how we define work.

Because at the end of the day, the burnout generation isn't lazy, entitled, or unmotivated. We're just tired. And we're finally asking: *What if life didn't have to be this way?*

Part 3
The Systemic Issues Behind Hustle Culture

"Hustle culture was never about hard work—it was about control. Corporations convinced us that burnout is a personal weakness rather than a structural issue, so they could replace fair wages with 'wellness perks' and call exploitation 'flexibility.' The real scam isn't that we're not working hard enough—it's that we were ever told we had to work this hard to survive."

Chapter 7

The Corporate Wellness Scam – When Self-Care is a Productivity Tool

"Have You Tried Yoga?"

It happens like clockwork. Employees are overworked, stressed, and barely holding it together, so what does the company do? Offer a mindfulness workshop. Maybe an office-wide yoga session. Maybe they'll throw in a mental health day—right after reminding you that your workload won't change, and your deadlines are still the same.

The message is clear: *Your exhaustion isn't a result of our unrealistic expectations—it's your mindset that needs fixing.*

Corporate wellness programs were supposed to be about making work healthier, but in reality, they've become **a tool to keep employees functioning just enough to keep working**. Instead of addressing the root causes of burnout—long hours, low wages, toxic workplace culture—companies have found a more convenient solution: turning "self-care" into a **corporate performance metric**.

Because if you're still stressed after your meditation break, that's *your* problem, not theirs.

How Mindfulness, Yoga, and "Wellness Perks" Became Productivity Hacks

There's nothing inherently wrong with mindfulness, meditation, or wellness initiatives. The problem is **how companies use them**—not as genuine acts of care, but as **Band-Aids for structural problems.**

Instead of offering **higher salaries**, they offer **snack stations**.

Instead of giving employees **reasonable workloads**, they give them **stress management workshops**.

Instead of **hiring more staff**, they encourage **"resilience training"** so workers can learn to cope with the burnout they created.

It's all about optics. Companies want to *look* like they care without making any real sacrifices. And why would they? Actually fixing workplace stress would mean acknowledging **their role** in creating it.

But it gets worse—because in many workplaces, engaging with these wellness programs isn't just an option, it's an **expectation**. Employees are encouraged (or outright pressured) to participate in these programs, subtly shifting the responsibility of burnout **away from management and onto the individual.**

You're exhausted? **Have you tried gratitude journaling?**

Feeling overwhelmed? **Maybe you should meditate more.**

Struggling with impossible deadlines? **A quick mindfulness session should do the trick.**

In this setup, the company never has to change. The solution to burnout is framed as **personal self-improvement**, not a **systemic problem**.

Why Companies Choose Perks Over Pay

If a company truly wanted to improve employee well-being, the solutions are simple:

- **Higher wages** (because financial stress is one of the biggest causes of anxiety).

- **Reasonable workloads** (so employees don't have to sacrifice their health to meet deadlines).

- **Flexible work arrangements** (so people aren't forced to be "always on").

- **Stronger labor protections** (so employees have actual recourse when mistreated).

But those things cost money. And companies don't want to spend money on their workforce when they can get away with spending *less*.

That's why they invest in "culture" instead of compensation. It's cheaper to install a nap pod than to **offer paid sick leave**. It's easier to run a wellness seminar than to **provide fair maternity leave or mental health benefits**.

And because these wellness programs create the illusion of care, they **deflect criticism**. If you're struggling despite all these wonderful initiatives, it must mean *you're* not taking full advantage of them.

And that's the real scam—**burnout is repackaged as a personal failure rather than a systemic issue**.

Burnout Isn't a Mindset Problem—It's a Workplace Problem

The corporate wellness scam works because it **shifts the blame away from the employer**. It tells workers that their exhaustion is a sign of personal weakness, not the direct result of toxic work environments.

And it keeps us in the cycle.

- We feel burned out, so we turn to the company's wellness programs.

- The programs don't actually solve the problem, but they make it feel like help is available.

- We push through, believing that we just need to take better care of ourselves.

- We keep working, over and over, until we break.

At that point, one of two things happens: either we leave (and are replaced by someone new, ready to be thrown into the cycle), or we stay and accept that **this is just how it is**.

But it doesn't have to be.

. . .

Breaking the Cycle: What Real Change Looks Like

If companies actually cared about employee well-being, they wouldn't be pushing **mindfulness apps**—they'd be pushing for **structural change**. But since they won't, it's up to workers to **demand better**.

1 Recognize the scam. Wellness perks aren't a substitute for fair treatment. Don't let free snacks distract you from low wages.

2 Set boundaries. Burnout isn't something to "fix" with self-care—it's something to prevent with **actual work-life balance.**

3 Push for systemic change. Unionizing, collective bargaining, and policy changes will do more for workplace wellness than any yoga session ever could.

Because at the end of the day, the best way to reduce burnout **isn't more wellness perks—it's less bullshit.**

Chapter 8

The Gig Economy Trap – Freedom or Just More Exploitation?

"Be Your Own Boss" (And Work Twice as Hard for Half the Pay)

It sounds like a dream: No bosses, no rigid schedules, no soul-crushing 9-to-5. Just you, your laptop, and the freedom to work whenever, wherever, and however you want. The gig economy promised independence, flexibility, and unlimited earning potential.

But here's the truth: **it was never about freedom—it was about shifting risk from corporations onto workers.**

The rise of freelancing, gig work, and the so-called "creator economy" was sold to us as the future of work. But in reality, it's just old-school exploitation in new, shinier packaging. Companies figured out that instead of hiring full-time employees with benefits and protections, they could turn *everyone* into an "independent contractor" and save billions.

And now? Millions of workers are trapped in an economy

where they're technically their own boss—but somehow **still struggling to make ends meet**.

The Illusion of Autonomy

The gig economy runs on one seductive idea: **freedom**.

You get to choose your hours. You get to work for yourself. You don't have to answer to anyone.

Except... none of that is really true.

• Rideshare drivers might set their own schedules, but **they don't control how much they get paid** (Uber and Lyft adjust wages with algorithmic precision to keep drivers working more for less).

• Freelancers can pick their own projects, but **they still have to fight for gigs in an oversaturated market** (and often get undercut by lower bids).

• Delivery workers technically work "whenever they want," but **peak hours and demand-based pay force them to work at inconvenient times just to break even**.

The freedom of gig work is an illusion. Most gig workers aren't independent entrepreneurs—they're **low-cost, disposable labor** for companies that refuse to hire employees.

And the best part for corporations? They don't owe you anything.

No benefits.

No paid time off.

No job security.

If business is slow? **That's your problem.**

If you get sick? **Figure it out.**

If the app changes the payment structure and suddenly you're making less? **Too bad.**

The companies hold all the power. And the workers? They're on their own.

How Companies Shifted Risk to Workers (And Called It "Flexibility")

For decades, corporations bore the responsibility of employing workers. They had to provide benefits, pay into unemployment insurance, and follow labor laws that protected employees. But as gig platforms exploded, companies realized they could **offload all that responsibility onto workers themselves.**

They started calling workers **"independent contractors"** instead of employees. And with that simple change, they no longer had to:

- Provide healthcare or retirement benefits.

- Guarantee a stable paycheck.

- Offer paid sick leave or vacation days.

- Follow basic labor protections like minimum wage laws.

They turned work into a **pay-per-task** system, where workers are constantly hustling for the next gig, the next client, the next payday.

And for many, that means working longer hours **just to make what used to be a livable wage**.

- A study found that **many Uber and Lyft drivers make less than minimum wage** after expenses.

- Gig workers have no safety net—**if they're deactivated from a platform, they lose their entire income overnight**.

- Freelancers often deal with **unpaid invoices, inconsistent pay, and no recourse when clients ghost them**.

Yet, despite all this, gig companies still frame it as **a choice**.

They tell workers:

"You don't have to do this. You can always quit."

As if most gig workers have the financial cushion to just walk away.

Because the reality is, for many, gig work isn't a choice. It's the only option left.

The Financial Instability of "Being Your Own Boss"

The most dangerous part of the gig economy is that **workers bear all the financial risk**—and companies get to sit back and profit.

Traditional employees have at least some stability: they know how much they'll make each paycheck. They get health insurance. They have legal protections.

Gig workers, on the other hand, are at the mercy of **market demand, fluctuating pay rates, and unpredictable workloads.**

• Uber drivers don't get to negotiate their fares—**the app decides how much they make, and it changes constantly.**

• Delivery workers don't control how many orders they get—**they just have to hope there's enough work to go around.**

• Freelancers can't guarantee steady income—**one bad month can wipe out their savings.**

And then there's **the hidden costs of gig work:**

• Rideshare drivers pay for their own gas, maintenance, and insurance.

• Freelancers have to handle their own taxes, healthcare, and retirement savings.

• Many gig workers spend **unpaid time** searching for work, negotiating rates, and dealing with administrative tasks.

At the end of the day, **many gig workers end up making less than minimum wage** when you factor in expenses and unpaid labor.

But the companies don't care—because **they've already gotten what they wanted**: a massive, disposable workforce that they can exploit without consequence.

Can Gig Work Ever Be Sustainable?

Despite all of this, gig work isn't going away. In fact, it's expanding. More and more industries are moving toward contract-based, temporary work models. Even white-collar jobs—graphic design, marketing, consulting—are being "gigified."

So, the question isn't whether gig work will survive—it's whether it can be **made fair.**

What would a *just* gig economy look like?

1 Worker Protections – Gig workers should be classified as employees **or** given legal protections like health insurance, paid leave, and unemployment benefits.

2 Fair Pay Standards – Minimum wage laws should apply to gig workers, ensuring that their hourly earnings (after expenses) meet livable wage standards.

3 Transparency – Companies should be required to disclose how pay is determined, so workers aren't blindsided by sudden rate changes.

4 Collective Bargaining – Gig workers should have the right to unionize and negotiate better conditions.

Because **flexibility shouldn't come at the cost of stability**.

Freedom shouldn't mean **"you're on your own"**—it should mean **having control over your work without sacrificing security**.

And until that happens, the gig economy isn't about empowerment.

It's about **exploitation with better branding.**

Chapter 9

Who Wins from Hustle Culture? (Hint: Not Us)

The People Profiting from Our Exhaustion

Every time we push through exhaustion to answer one more email, work one more shift, or grind for one more opportunity, someone is benefiting.

Spoiler: **it's not us.**

Hustle culture doesn't exist in a vacuum. It's not some accidental phenomenon—it's a carefully crafted system designed to **extract as much labor as possible while giving as little in return.** The billionaires telling us to work harder? The companies pushing for "passion-driven" work? The influencers romanticizing the grind? They're all profiting from a system that convinces *us* to accept burnout as normal.

Because the truth is, hustle culture isn't about making *us* successful. It's about making **them** richer.

The Billionaires Selling the "Hard Work" Myth

Elon Musk says, *"Nobody ever changed the world on 40 hours a week."*

Jeff Bezos preaches about the importance of work ethic.

Corporate leaders praise employees who go "above and beyond."

And yet, **these are the same people who don't actually do the grinding themselves.**

Let's be clear: billionaires don't work 100-hour weeks. They might put in long hours *early on*, but once they reach the top, their wealth multiplies *without* their labor. They invest, they delegate, they outsource. Meanwhile, they convince the rest of us that *if we're not succeeding, it's because we're not working hard enough.*

It's the perfect con.

Billionaires didn't get rich by working harder than everyone else. They got rich by:

• **Paying workers as little as possible** while pocketing the profits.

• **Encouraging unpaid labor** (internships, "for exposure" gigs, side hustles that never pay off).

• **Repackaging exploitation as opportunity** (calling low wages "experience" and excessive hours "dedication").

They rely on a system where people feel *guilty* for resting. A system where overwork is normalized, because **exhausted workers don't have the energy to fight back.**

And as long as we believe the myth that success is just a matter of *grinding harder*, the cycle continues.

The Unpaid Labor Behind Hustle Culture

Let's talk about all the work that keeps industries running—but doesn't get properly paid.

1. Emotional Labor

In many industries, workers aren't just expected to do their job—they're expected to **manage emotions, diffuse tension, and absorb stress**.

• Service workers are expected to **smile and stay polite** even when customers are abusive.

• Employees (especially women) are pressured to be **peacemakers in toxic workplaces**.

• Workers are expected to **go the extra mile** for "company culture," even if it means unpaid emotional labor.

This isn't in the job description. It's not compensated. But companies **expect it anyway**.

2. "Exposure" Work and the Free Labor Economy

Another scam? Convincing people to work for free in exchange for **"opportunity."**

• **Unpaid internships** that only people with financial privilege can afford to take.

• **Freelancers being told to work for "exposure."**

- **Artists and creatives constantly being asked for free work** because it will "build their portfolio."

Companies love free labor. And as long as they can convince people that *working for free today will lead to paid work tomorrow*, they will continue exploiting ambition.

3. The Work Women and Marginalized Groups Are Expected to Do for Free

There's a reason burnout disproportionately affects **women, people of color, and marginalized workers**. They're often expected to do **extra, unpaid work** on top of their actual job:

- **Diversity and inclusion efforts** (without extra pay).

- **Mentorship and emotional support** for colleagues.

- **Household labor and caregiving** on top of full-time work.

And when they burn out? They're told they should've managed their time better.

The Growing Wealth Gap and the Meritocracy Lie

Hustle culture runs on one central belief: **if you work hard enough, you'll succeed.**

But here's the truth: **success isn't just about effort—it's about access.**

Hard work alone doesn't guarantee success when:

- **The starting line isn't the same for everyone.** A billionaire's son and a first-generation college student don't have the same obstacles.

- **Wealth is self-replicating.** Money creates money—people who start with wealth have a built-in safety net, investment opportunities, and financial literacy.

- **Wages stay low while costs rise.** Millennials and Gen Z aren't lazy—they're just **earning less while paying more for housing, education, and healthcare.**

Despite what hustle culture tells us, **most people aren't failing because they aren't trying hard enough—they're failing because the system is stacked against them.**

So, Who Wins?

The short answer? **The people at the top.**

Billionaires.

CEOs.

Corporations that maximize profits by keeping wages low and expectations high.

Hustle culture benefits the people who **extract labor while avoiding responsibility.** It convinces workers that if they just push a little harder, they'll finally "make it"—while the real winners sit back and profit from everyone else's exhaustion.

So what's the alternative?

Rejecting the Hustle and Reclaiming Our Time

1 Stop glorifying overwork. Working yourself to the bone is not a badge of honor—it's a sign that something is broken.

2 Recognize that burnout isn't a personal failure. You're not weak. You're not lazy. You're in a system designed to keep you grinding.

3 Push for systemic change. Higher wages, stronger labor protections, and **a cultural shift that values people over profits**—these are the real solutions.

Because at the end of the day, the question isn't whether hustle culture works.

It's **who it works for.**

And until we stop playing by its rules, the answer will never be *us*.

Part 4
The Future of Work and Rest

"Rest is not a reward for hard work—it is a right. For too long, we've measured success by exhaustion, productivity by self-sacrifice. But the future of work isn't about grinding harder; it's about reclaiming our time, redefining success, and finally choosing to live."

Chapter 10

The Anti-Hustle Movement – How We're Fighting Back

The Moment the System Started Cracking

For years, hustle culture felt like an inescapable force—something we had to accept, no matter how exhausted, underpaid, or overworked we were. We were told that if we weren't succeeding, we just needed to grind harder, sacrifice more, and push through.

But then, something changed. People started saying *no*.

The Great Resignation, quiet quitting, the rise of worker solidarity—these aren't random trends. They're **acts of resistance** against a system that demands everything and gives little in return. They're proof that workers—especially Millennials and Gen Z—are no longer willing to accept burnout as a normal part of life.

We've been conditioned to think that work should define us. That success is tied to how much we produce. That exhaustion is a sign of ambition. But slowly, people are realizing that **hustle culture was never for us**—and now, they're pushing back.

So, what does the future of work actually look like? And what happens when people finally stop playing by the rules of a broken system?

The Great Resignation and Quiet Quitting: Opting Out of Exploitation

The Great Resignation wasn't just about people quitting their jobs—it was about people quitting the lie.

For decades, companies have underpaid employees, cut benefits, and pushed unrealistic workloads while increasing profits for those at the top. But in 2021, something unexpected happened: **workers walked away.**

Millions of employees across industries—hospitality, retail, tech, healthcare—quit in search of something better. Some switched careers. Others left traditional jobs entirely. And for the first time in a long time, companies had to scramble to retain workers, offering higher wages, better benefits, and actual incentives to stay.

And for those who didn't quit? **There was quiet quitting.**

Despite the misleading name, quiet quitting isn't about laziness—it's about **setting boundaries**. It's refusing to overwork without extra pay. It's saying no to unpaid emotional labor. It's rejecting the idea that our worth is tied to how much we produce.

And while corporate leaders panicked over these trends, calling workers "entitled" and "unmotivated," the truth is clear: **people are finally realizing their value.**

Why Gen Z is Rejecting Traditional Work Norms

No generation has called out the failures of hustle culture quite like Gen Z.

Unlike Millennials, who grew up with the "American Dream 2.0" lie (*work hard, get a degree, and you'll be rewarded*), Gen Z saw the system fail in real time. They watched their older siblings and parents burn out. They entered the workforce during economic instability, rising costs of living, and stagnant wages. And they aren't buying the hustle culture myth.

Instead, Gen Z is rewriting the rules:

• **They value flexibility over status.** They're more likely to demand remote work, flexible schedules, and work-life balance than previous generations.

• **They prioritize mental health.** They're not afraid to call out toxic work environments or leave jobs that compromise their well-being.

• **They aren't loyal to exploitative employers.** They job-hop more frequently, knowing that loyalty to a company rarely pays off.

Rather than trying to force themselves into broken work structures, Gen Z is **reshaping the workforce to fit them—** and older generations are starting to follow suit.

This shift isn't just cultural—it's structural. The very foundation of modern work is changing, and companies that don't adapt will be left behind.

The Rise of Anti-Capitalist Work Models

So if hustle culture is dying, what comes next?

For years, alternatives to traditional corporate structures have existed, but now they're gaining mainstream traction. More people are exploring **cooperative work models, labor unions, and shorter workweeks** as viable alternatives to burnout-driven capitalism.

1. Worker Cooperatives: Collective Ownership Instead of Corporate Greed

Unlike traditional companies, **worker co-ops** are owned and run by employees. There's no CEO hoarding wealth while workers struggle—**profits are shared**, and decisions are made collectively.

Worker co-ops exist across industries—from tech to food service to retail—offering a model where businesses can thrive **without exploiting their workers.**

2. Labor Unions: The Power of Collective Action

Unions are making a comeback, and for good reason. When workers organize, they gain the power to demand:

- Fair wages
- Better benefits
- Job security

- Protection from exploitation

We're seeing union victories in companies that historically resisted them—**Amazon, Starbucks, and Apple**—proving that even in modern capitalism, workers still have power when they come together.

3. The Four-Day Workweek: Productivity Without Burnout

One of the biggest shifts in work culture? The growing push for **four-day workweeks**. Studies show that working fewer hours **doesn't reduce productivity**—in fact, it improves it. Countries and companies experimenting with four-day weeks report:

- Higher efficiency
- Improved mental health
- Increased job satisfaction

It's proof that **we never needed 40+ hour workweeks in the first place**—we were just conditioned to believe that overwork was necessary.

What Comes Next?

The anti-hustle movement is about more than just quitting jobs or setting boundaries—it's about **fundamentally rethinking what work should be**.

It's about rejecting the idea that **we exist to be productive** and embracing the fact that **we deserve lives outside of labor.**

- **Work should support life, not consume it.**

- **Success should be about fulfillment, not exhaustion.**

- **Rest is not a luxury—it's a right.**

For too long, hustle culture made us believe that we had to earn our worth through suffering. That if we weren't constantly grinding, we weren't *enough*.

But people are waking up. They're refusing to settle for burnout. They're building new models of work that prioritize well-being over profit.

And slowly but surely, **the future of work is shifting.**

Chapter 11

Rest as Rebellion – The Radical Act of Doing Nothing

Why Does Rest Feel Like a Guilty Pleasure?

Try this: do absolutely nothing for ten minutes. No scrolling, no checking emails, no catching up on a side hustle. Just sit.

Feels weird, right?

That's because we've been conditioned to believe that **rest is a waste of time**. That slowing down means falling behind. That if we're not actively producing, optimizing, or improving, we're failing.

Hustle culture has robbed us of the ability to simply *be*. Rest isn't just discouraged—it's demonized. We hear it in the way people talk:

- "I'll sleep when I'm dead."
- "You have the same 24 hours as Beyoncé."
- "If you're not moving forward, you're falling behind."

This mindset is everywhere, and it keeps us trapped in an endless cycle of guilt whenever we try to slow down. But here's the truth: **rest isn't laziness. It's survival.**

And in a world that glorifies burnout, choosing to rest is nothing short of radical.

Reframing Laziness as Self-Preservation

Capitalism thrives on convincing us that we *always* need to be doing something. If we're not working, we should be working on ourselves—learning a new skill, improving our fitness, side-hustling our passions into profit.

But what if we refused?

What if we stopped believing that our worth is tied to our productivity? What if we redefined laziness—not as failure, but as **a necessary act of self-preservation**?

Because let's be real—hustle culture doesn't actually reward hard work. It rewards **exploitation**. It convinces people to push beyond their limits, then shames them when their bodies and minds collapse.

Rest isn't weakness—it's how we protect ourselves from a system that was never designed with our well-being in mind.

The Science of Rest: Why Doing Less Makes Us More Productive

Ironically, the very thing hustle culture discourages—**rest**—is what makes people more effective in the long run.

1. Rest Boosts Creativity

Some of the greatest breakthroughs in history came not from grinding, but from **stepping away**. Albert Einstein reportedly had his best ideas while daydreaming. Writers and artists throughout history have credited their creativity to long walks, naps, and unstructured time.

Our brains need **idle moments** to process information and form new ideas. Constant work doesn't lead to innovation—it leads to mental exhaustion.

2. Sleep is a Productivity Hack

Despite what corporate culture tells us, **sleep deprivation is not a badge of honor**. Lack of sleep:

- Lowers cognitive function
- Increases mistakes
- Weakens immune response
- Shortens lifespan

Meanwhile, well-rested people **perform better, think faster, and make fewer errors**. Hustle culture treats sleep as optional, but science proves it's **non-negotiable**.

3. The Brain Needs Downtime to Function Properly

Studies show that people who take **regular breaks** are more productive than those who grind non-stop. The Pomodoro Technique—working in short bursts with scheduled breaks—is based on the idea that **humans aren't designed to focus for long periods without rest**.

So why are we still pretending that overwork is a virtue?

Unlearning Hustle Culture: A Personal Reflection

For years, I believed rest was something I had to *earn*. I felt guilty for sleeping in, ashamed if I spent a day doing "nothing," and constantly anxious about whether I was working hard enough.

Even vacations felt stressful—I would bring my laptop, answer emails, and tell myself I was "relaxing" when in reality, I was still tethered to the grind.

It took **burnout** for me to realize the truth: I didn't need more discipline. I didn't need a better time-management strategy. **I needed to stop glorifying exhaustion.**

Rest isn't a reward for hard work. **It's a basic human need.**

And the more I started embracing rest—not just as a break, but as an essential part of life—the more I realized just how deeply hustle culture had infiltrated my mindset.

Choosing Rest is a Radical Act

In a society that profits off our exhaustion, rest is rebellion.

- Rest is refusing to define your worth by your productivity.
- Rest is rejecting the guilt that comes with slowing down.
- Rest is prioritizing your well-being over a system that never cared about you in the first place.

But choosing rest isn't always easy. We've been conditioned

to feel guilty about it, to justify it, to earn it. So let's start normalizing:

- **Taking breaks without feeling bad about it.**
- **Saying no to extra work that doesn't serve us.**
- **Unplugging without the fear of "falling behind."**
- **Sleeping without shame.**

Because the truth is, **we were never meant to run on empty.**

The most radical thing we can do in a world obsessed with productivity? **Rest. And not feel guilty about it.**

Chapter 12

Redefining Success – What Comes After the Grind?

If Success Isn't About Working Harder, Then What Is It?

For most of our lives, we've been told that success looks a certain way: a high-paying job, a prestigious title, a packed schedule, and the ability to "outwork" everyone else.

Hustle culture taught us that success is measured in **hours worked, promotions earned, and sacrifices made**. That if we just grind a little harder, we'll finally reach the top—wherever that is.

But what happens when we get there?

The reality is, many of us have checked the boxes. We've worked the long hours. We've chased promotions. We've hustled ourselves into exhaustion.

And still, **we don't feel successful—we just feel tired.**

So if grinding harder isn't the answer, then what is?

What if we stopped defining success by how much we produce—and started defining it by how much we actually **live**?

Decoupling Self-Worth from Productivity

One of the biggest lies hustle culture sells us is that our **value as people** is tied to how much we achieve. That we are only as good as our output, our efficiency, our ability to monetize every moment.

But if that were true, then wouldn't the hardest-working people in society be the most successful? Wouldn't teachers, nurses, janitors, and caregivers—who work tirelessly every day—be the wealthiest, most celebrated people in the world?

Instead, **the richest people are often the ones who work the least.**

We have to stop pretending that overwork equals worth. That exhaustion is a measure of ambition. That success is something we can only claim if we've suffered enough to "deserve" it.

Because the truth is, **you are valuable even when you're resting.** You matter even when you're not producing.

And if we truly want to redefine success, we have to start by rejecting the idea that it has to be **earned** through burnout.

Imagining a World Where Work Isn't Everything

For too long, we've been stuck in a model where work **dominates** our lives, leaving little time for anything else. But what if we flipped the equation? What if work wasn't the **center** of our identity, but just one part of a full, meaningful life?

A world where success is measured not in **grind hours**, but in **quality of life**.

Where instead of asking, *"What do you do?"* we ask, *"What makes you happy?"*

Where time spent with family, creative projects, community involvement, and mental well-being **matter just as much as career milestones.**

And yes, we still need to work to survive in the current system. But what if we started treating work as **just that**—a way to support life, rather than something that consumes it?

Because at the end of the day, no one looks back on their life and thinks, *I wish I had worked more weekends.*

They think about the people they loved. The experiences they had. The moments that made them feel **alive.**

That is success.

What Comes After the Grind?

If we're rejecting hustle culture, we need to replace it with something better.

So what does post-hustle success look like?

1. Success as Balance

Success doesn't mean constant achievement—it means **having time for what matters**. Time for family, for creativity, for personal growth, for rest.

2. Success as Well-Being

Mental and physical health shouldn't be sacrificed for a paycheck. True success means **having the energy to enjoy life—not just survive it.**

3. Success as Community

Individual success means nothing if it comes at the expense of others. Instead of competing in a toxic rat race, we can **build systems that uplift everyone—through fair wages, worker rights, and collective care.**

4. Success as Freedom

Real success isn't working nonstop to make someone else richer. It's having the **autonomy** to shape your own life, on your own terms.

Redefining Success—On Our Own Terms

For so long, we've accepted someone else's definition of success—a definition that serves **corporations, billionaires, and a system designed to keep us working endlessly.**

But we don't have to play by those rules anymore.

Success is not about suffering.

Success is not about exhaustion.

Success is not about being the last one at the office or the first one to reply to an email at midnight.

Success is **whatever we decide it is.**

So let's redefine it—collectively, intentionally, and in a way that actually makes life **worth living.**

Conclusion: The Death of Hustle Culture?

Is Hustle Culture Finally Dying?

For years, hustle culture was seen as the ultimate blueprint for success. The grind was glorified. Productivity was a badge of honor. Overwork was the norm.

But something has shifted. People are questioning the system. They're quitting, setting boundaries, and rejecting the idea that success must come at the cost of their well-being.

So, is hustle culture dying?

Not yet.

The corporate world is still invested in keeping people overworked, underpaid, and too exhausted to fight back. Productivity myths still dominate our conversations about work. Burnout is still widespread.

But here's the good news: **we don't have to wait for hustle culture to die—we can kill it ourselves.**

Conclusion: The Death of Hustle Culture?

The question isn't just *is hustle culture ending?* It's *what comes next?*

Because the future of work isn't something we passively inherit—it's something we build.

Where Do We Go from Here?

If we want to move beyond hustle culture, we have to stop playing by its rules. That means unlearning everything we were taught about work, success, and self-worth.

1. Reject the Idea That Busyness = Value

We've been conditioned to equate packed schedules with importance. But **being busy isn't the same as being fulfilled**. Start measuring success in joy, rest, and meaningful connections—not just output.

2. Push Back Against Toxic Work Norms

Companies won't change unless they're forced to. Demand better. Advocate for fair wages, reasonable hours, and humane working conditions. If you have the ability to, support unions and labor movements that fight for worker rights.

3. Normalize Rest (Without Guilt)

Rest is not something you *earn*—it's something you *deserve*. Stop apologizing for taking time off. Stop glorifying burnout. Rest isn't a sign of laziness; it's a sign of self-respect.

4. Redefine Success on Your Own Terms

If success isn't about grinding yourself into the ground, then what is it about? Define success in a way that actually serves you. Maybe it's about balance. Maybe it's about freedom.

Conclusion: The Death of Hustle Culture?

Maybe it's about having the time and energy to do things that make life feel meaningful.

A Call to Action: Building a New Culture of Work, Rest, and Success

The fight against hustle culture isn't just about quitting toxic jobs or working fewer hours—it's about **building a world where work doesn't define our entire existence**.

That means:

- **Pushing for systemic change**—higher wages, fair labor laws, and protections for workers.
- **Normalizing work-life balance**—rejecting guilt for resting, taking breaks, and valuing free time.
- **Redefining ambition**—not as endless productivity, but as the pursuit of a meaningful, balanced life.

We don't have to accept a world where burnout is the price of success. We don't have to live lives dictated by someone else's definition of achievement.

Hustle culture only survives if we continue to feed it.

So let's starve it. Let's step away from the grind. Let's reclaim our time, our rest, and our lives.

Because real success?

It isn't about working more.

It's about living *better*.